7.9
/1.0

#30995

Civil War Generals

by

Dan Harmon

Chelsea House Publishers

CHELSEA HOUSE PUBLISHERS

Editor-in-Chief Stephen Reginald
Managing Editor James D. Gallagher
Production Manager Pamela Loos
Art Director Sara Davis
Picture Editor Judy Hasday
Senior Production Editor Lisa Chippendale
Designers Takeshi Takahashi, Keith Trego

First Printing

1 3 5 7 9 8 6 4 2

Library of Congress Cataloging-in-Publication Data

Harmon, Dan.
Civil War generals / by Dan Harmon.

    p. cm. — (Looking into the past)
Includes bibliographical references and index.
Summary: Examines some of the generals who led the
Union and Confederate forces in the Civil War, including
Beauregard, Burnside, and Stonewall Jackson.

ISBN 0-7910-4675-3
1. Generals—United States—Biography—Juvenile literature.
2. Generals—Confederate States of America—Biography—
Juvenile literature. 3. United States. Army—Biography—
Juvenile literature. 4. Confederate States of America. Army—
Biography—Juvenile literature. 5. United States—History—
Civil War, 1861-1865—Biography—Juvenile literature. [1.
Generals. 2. United States—History—Civil War, 1861-
1865—Biography.] I. Title. II. Series.
E467.H27 1997
973.7'092'2—dc21   97-35674
[B]   CIP
                                                             AC

CONTENTS

CULTURE, CUSTOMS, AND RITUALS

The important moments of our lives—from birth through puberty, aging, and death—are made more meaningful by culture, customs, and rituals. But what is culture? The word *culture*, broadly defined, includes the way of life of an entire society. This encompasses customs, rituals, codes of manners, dress, languages, norms of behavior, and systems of beliefs. Individuals are both acted on by and react to a culture—and so generate new cultural forms and customs.

What is custom? Custom refers to accepted social practices that separate one cultural group from another. Every culture contains basic customs, often known as rites of transition or passage. These rites, or ceremonies, occur at different stages of life, from birth to death, and are sometimes religious in nature. In all cultures of the world today, a new baby is greeted and welcomed into its family through ceremony. Some ceremonies, such as the bar mitzvah, a religious initiation for teenage Jewish boys, mark the transition from childhood to adulthood. Marriage also is usually celebrated by a ritual of some sort. Death is another rite of transition. All known cultures contain beliefs about life after death, and all observe funeral rites and mourning customs.

What is a ritual? What is a rite? These terms are used interchangeably to describe a ceremony associated with a custom. The English ritual of shaking hands in greeting, for example, has become part of that culture. The washing of one's hands could be considered a ritual which helps a person achieve an accepted level of cleanliness—a requirement of the cultural beliefs that person holds.

The books in this series, *Looking into the Past: People,*

Places, and Customs, explore many of the most interesting rituals of different cultures through time. For example, did you know that in the year A.D. 1075 William the Conqueror ordered that a "Couvre feu" bell be rung at sunset in each town and city of England, as a signal to put out all fires? Because homes were made of wood and had thatched roofs, the bell served as a precaution against house fires. Today, this custom is no longer observed as it was 900 years ago, but the modern word *curfew* derives from its practice.

Another ritual that dates from centuries long past is the Japanese Samurai Festival. This colorful celebration commemorates the feats of the ancient samurai warriors who ruled the country hundreds of years ago. Japanese citizens dress in costumes, and direct descendants of warriors wear samurai swords during the festival. The making of these swords actually is a separate religious rite in itself.

Different cultures develop different customs. For example, people of different nations have developed various interesting ways to greet each other. In China 100 years ago, the ordinary salutation was a ceremonious, but not deep, bow, with the greeting "Kin t'ien ni hao ma?" (Are you well today?). During the same era, citizens of the Indian Ocean island nation Ceylon (now called Sri Lanka) greeted each other by placing their palms together with the fingers extended. When greeting a person of higher social rank, the hands were held in front of the forehead and the head was inclined.

Some symbols and rituals rooted in ancient beliefs are common to several cultures. For example, in China, Japan, and many of the countries of the East, a tortoise is a symbol of protection from black magic, while fish have represented fertility, new life, and prosperity since the beginnings of human civilization. Other ancient fertility symbols have been incorporated into religions we still practice today, and so these ancient beliefs remain a part of our civilization. A more recent belief, the legend of Santa Claus, is the story of a kind benefactor who brings gifts to the good children of the world. This story appears in the lore of nearly every nation. Each country developed its own variation on the legend and each celebrates Santa's arrival in a different way.

New rituals are being created all the time. On April 21, 1997, for example, the cremated remains of 24 people were launched into orbit around Earth on a Pegasus rocket. Included among the group whose ashes now head toward their "final frontier" are Gene Roddenberry, creator of the television series *Star Trek,* and Timothy Leary, a countercultural icon of the 1960s. Each person's remains were placed in a separate aluminum capsule engraved with the person's name and a commemorative phrase. The remains will orbit the Earth every 90 minutes for two to ten years. When the rocket does re-enter Earth's atmosphere, it will burn up with a great burst of light. This first-time ritual could become an accepted rite of passage, a custom in our culture that would supplant the current ceremonies marking the transition between life and death.

Curiosity about different customs, rites, and rituals dates back to the mercantile Greeks of classical times. Herodotus (484–425 B.C.), known as the "Father of History," described Egyptian culture. The Roman historian Tacitus (A.D. 55–117) similarly wrote a lengthy account about the customs of the "modern" European barbarians. From the Greeks to Marco Polo, from Columbus to the Pacific voyages of Captain James Cook, cultural differences have fascinated the literate world. The books in the *Looking into the Past* series collect the most interesting customs from many cultures of the past and explain their origins, meanings, and relationship to the present day.

In the future, space travel may very well provide the impetus for new cultures, customs, and rituals, which will in turn enthrall and interest the peoples of future millennia.

Fred L. Israel
The City College of the City University of New York

CONTRIBUTORS

Senior Consulting Editor FRED L. ISRAEL is an award-winning historian. He received the Scribe's Award from the American Bar Association for his work on the Chelsea House series *The Justices of the United States Supreme Court.* A specialist in early American history, he was general editor for Chelsea's *1897 Sears Roebuck Catalog.* Dr. Israel has also worked in association with Dr. Arthur M. Schlesinger, jr. on many projects, including *The History of U.S. Presidential Elections* and *The History of U.S. Political Parties.* They are currently working together on the Chelsea House series *The World 100 Years Ago,* which looks at the traditions, customs, and cultures of many nations at the turn of the century.

DAN HARMON is a freelance editor and writer in Charleston, South Carolina—where the Civil War began with the bombardment of Fort Sumter in 1861. He has written three books on humor and history and has written historical and cultural articles for the *New York Times, Music Journal, Nautilus,* and more than a score of other periodicals. He is the managing editor of *Sandlapper: The Magazine of South Carolina* and is editor of *The Lawyer's PC* computer newsletter. His special interests are Christian and nautical history, folk music, and correspondence chess.

Generals of the Civil War

T he generals who led the Union and Confederate forces in the American Civil War were a fascinating lot. They came from many walks of life: farmers, lawyers, planters, politicians, and shopkeepers. Some were outstanding cadets at West Point who turned out to be disappointing field commanders. Others were mediocre students who later shone brilliantly in action. Many of these leaders had been tested in the Mexican War and Indian campaigns, but none had faced a combat as vast or complex as the Civil War.

Remarkably, the fraternity of officers who divided themselves at the war's outbreak remained friends, in many instances, during and after the war. They had trained and fought together and introduced each other to future brides. Generals on one side sometimes had close relatives leading the other. On occasion, they had more respect for their old comrades across the lines of battle than they had for their own wartime colleagues.

For some, like the Union's Ulysses S. Grant and Philip H. Sheridan or the Confederacy's Robert E. Lee and Stonewall Jackson, the war established or solidified their reputations. For others, the war ended their careers. Each of the leaders, however, contributed in some way to the nation's hour of terrible crisis.

Although the years 1861–65 were the worst of times, America survived the Civil War and ultimately emerged stronger than ever before. The war is part of our history, dreadful but rich in stories of bravery and heroism. It was a fiery furnace that helped temper the United States into a strong nation, a truly independent union.

These are a few of the leaders who served in the furnace.

GEN. P.G.T. BEAUREGARD.

P. G. T.
BEAUREGARD

Pierre Gustave Toutant Beauregard saw action in more varied places than most Civil War generals. He commanded the Confederate bombardment of Fort Sumter in Charleston Harbor, South Carolina—the engagement that started the war in April 1861. Three months later, he was second-in-command of the Southerners at the First Battle of Bull Run in Virginia. The next year he served in the western campaign, most notably at Shiloh in Tennessee. In 1863–64, he was back in Charleston, commanding the city's defense against a Union blockade. Then, near the war's end, he returned to Virginia to serve under Gen. Robert E. Lee.

Beauregard was born in Louisiana to Creole parents in 1818. French was his first language. At 20 he graduated near the top of his class from West Point. Like many future Civil War generals on both sides, he distinguished himself as an officer in the Mexican War in the late 1840s. He was wounded twice there and was promoted for his gallantry.

Because of his victories at Fort Sumter and Bull Run, Beauregard became one of the Civil War's most famous generals early in the conflict. However, many Southerners thought he should have annihilated the Union army at Bull Run by pursuing the routed bluecoats. His own men actually were too tired and disorganized to fight any longer. Nevertheless, Confederate president Jefferson Davis soon replaced Beauregard and, following an illness, Beauregard was relegated to secondary commands.

After the war, Beauregard became president of a railroad, refusing offers to command the armies of Egypt and Rumania. He died at New Orleans in 1893.

GEN.A.E.BURNSIDE.

A. E. BURNSIDE

Ambrose E. Burnside not only was a Union leader, he was a respected firearms manufacturer who invented one of the most popular rifles used by his army.

Born in Indiana in 1824, Burnside was educated at West Point. He fought against Mexicans and Apaches in the Southwest, then resigned from the U.S. Army to become a carbine maker in Rhode Island. Ultimately, more than 55,000 of his rifles would be used during the Civil War.

Burnside entered the war as a colonel. He was promoted to brigadier general after the First Battle of Bull Run.

By late 1862, President Abraham Lincoln was disappointed in the leadership of Gen. George McClellan, commander of the Army of the Potomac, and offered Burnside command of the army. Twice Burnside refused, but in November 1862 he accepted. He held the post only a few months, though. His poor decisions resulted in defeat at Fredericksburg, and he was replaced by Gen. Joseph Hooker.

Burnside served in various command roles in Tennessee and Virginia. Sometimes he led well; on other occasions he failed. Through it all, he remained popular with fellow officers—blue and gray alike. It is said Confederate leaders privately mourned the humiliation of their former comrade at Fredericksburg. After the destruction of his unit at the Battle of the Crater, Burnside was relieved of his command. He resigned from military service several days after Lee's surrender at Appomattox.

Despite his mediocre war record, Burnside was elected governor of Rhode Island, then a U.S. senator representing that state. He died in 1881 at Bristol, Rhode Island.

GEN. BENJAMIN F. BUTLER

BENJAMIN F. BUTLER

A noted strategist while serving as a Union officer, Benjamin Franklin Butler also was a famous statesman before and after the Civil War. This lawyer, legislator, and Democratic National Convention delegate in 1860 tried to calm secession frenzy. He went so far as to support Jefferson Davis' nomination for U.S. president, realizing that a moderate Southern candidate stood the best chance of keeping the nation united.

Butler, born in 1818 in New Hampshire, performed his finest Civil War service during the early stage of the conflict. He led a successful invasion unit against the North Carolina coast in 1861. When New Orleans surrendered in 1862, he was appointed occupational governor of Louisiana. His administration was effective, although critics accused him of corruption and heavy-handedness.

He later had a disappointing military record in Virginia and North Carolina. Gen. Ulysses S. Grant relieved him of command before the war ended. Like many "citizen generals" (commanders of volunteer units, as opposed to West Point professionals), Butler did not rate highly in the eyes of career officers. Union admiral David Dixon Porter especially was frustrated by Butler's performance during the army and navy's difficult joint attack on Fort Fisher in 1864. Porter wrote angrily to Gen. William T. Sherman, "God save me from further connections with such generals."

Returning to politics, Butler was a U.S. congressman for more than a decade. He later was elected governor of Massachusetts, but his 1884 bid for the presidency failed. Butler died nine years later in Washington, D.C.

GEN. J. A. EARLY.

J. A. EARLY

In his mid-40s when the war began, Jubal Anderson Early was an "old man" among the Civil War generals. Like many officers on both sides of the conflict, the Virginia lawyer and West Point graduate actively opposed secession. But when his state broke from the Union, he joined the Confederate army as a colonel. He played a significant role in the Confederate victory at the First Battle of Bull Run, then was wounded at Williamsburg.

Early fought in most of the major battles with Lee's Army of Northern Virginia, rising to the rank of lieutenant general. "Old Jube" was dispatched by Lee to invade the North in the summer of 1864, late in the war. He defeated Gen. Lew Wallace's troops at Monocacy, Maryland, in July of that year. Two days later his army threatened Washington, D.C., until Union forces arrived, forcing the Rebels to withdraw. Early's foray succeeded in diverting many Yankee units from the main army that was pitted against Lee.

A series of defeats began a few months later at the hands of Union Gen. Philip Sheridan in the Shenandoah Valley. Early's portion of the dwindling Confederate army was scattered by Gen. George Custer, who later would earn glory and infamy as an Indian fighter. Increasingly unpopular in Southern newspaper accounts, Early was relieved of his command by Lee in March 1865, a month before the war's end.

Early fled to Mexico, then Canada, after the South surrendered. Eventually he returned to law practice in Lynchburg, Virginia. The first president of the Southern Historical Society, he died in Lynchburg in 1894.

GEN. R. S. EWELL.

R. S.
EWELL

any people think Civil War generals and their staffs commanded the war from distant hill-tops, watching the violence through bin-oculars. At times this was so, but high-level officers also engaged in actual fighting.

Confederate Gen. Richard Stoddert Ewell was one example. Born in 1817, Ewell was a decorated fighter on the southwestern frontier before the war. The Washington, D.C., native and West Point graduate then became a leading officer in Lee's army. He succeeded Stonewall Jackson as commander of the Confederate Second Corps after Jackson's death in 1863.

At the Battle of Groveton, Ewell lost a leg. Back in action with a wooden leg, he had his men strap him atop a horse so he could lead his unit into Pennsylvania in 1863. That drive resulted in the devastating Confederate defeat at Gettysburg. To some critics, Ewell was largely responsible for the loss because of his decision not to take the strategic Cemetery Hill early in the fighting.

Ewell was wounded again at the Battle of Kelly's Ford. He fell from his horse at the Battle of Spotsylvania Court House and was unable to return to field command.

Ewell was placed in charge of the defense of Richmond late in the war. He was captured days before Lee's surrender in April 1865 and was imprisoned in Massachusetts. Upon release, he settled on a farm in Spring Hill, Tennessee, where he died in 1872.

GEN. U. S. GRANT.

U. S. GRANT

President Lincoln seemed both blessed and cursed as he undertook the task of restoring the Union. From the beginning the Union had many more soldiers than the Confederacy. But the Northern leaders were overly cautious and slow to act. In battle after battle they lost when they should have won. They repeatedly were surprised and outmaneuvered, and they let opportunities for decisive victories slip away.

Not until spring 1864—a year before the war ended—did Lincoln find a worthy commander for the Union armies. Ulysses S. Grant of Ohio had an uneven military record, winning honors and promotions during the Mexican War, then being almost court-martialed. He was working as a clerk in Illinois when the war broke out. But after volunteering his services as a Union officer, his career flourished. He first served in the western campaigns, figuring prominently at the Battle of Shiloh and the siege of Vicksburg.

Lincoln made him a lieutenant general and named him general in chief of all the Union forces in March 1864. Grant directed the Northern armies until the war's end, forcing Lee to surrender at Appomattox, Virginia, on April 12, 1865. Two weeks later, Confederate Gen. Joseph E. Johnston surrendered his western army to Gen. William T. Sherman.

Grant was elected president of the United States in 1868; he was reelected in 1872. Unfortunately, his administration is remembered for its corruption. Mark Twain published Grant's *Personal Memoirs* in 1885—a book that sold extremely well and earned broad respect as a war record. Grant died of throat cancer in New York shortly after completing the book.

GEN. H. W. HALLECK.

H. W.
HALLECK

enry Wager Halleck was a man of law and letters before the war. Born in 1815 at Westernville, New York, he was a scholar who finished third in his class at West Point. He taught at the academy, lectured, traveled, and wrote books about military science. During the Mexican War, he served in the military government of California. He then resigned from the army and became one of California's leading lawyers. Halleck also wrote other books and was a wealthy man by the beginning of the Civil War.

President Lincoln appointed him a major general at the war's outset. "Old Brains," as Halleck was called by his colleagues, was assigned to a high post in the western theater. He held rank over many capable officers, including Ulysses S. Grant, John Pope, and D.C. Buell. Halleck himself proved to be an excellent administrative officer, but a terrible field commander. He was criticized for allowing vastly outnumbered Confederate forces to escape from Corinth, Mississippi, in 1862.

Although Secretary of the Navy Gideon Welles labeled Halleck "good for nothing" and Gen. George McClellan called him "hopelessly stupid" as a commander, Halleck's organizational accomplishments were undeniable. Lincoln named Halleck general in chief of the Union army in July 1862, and he served in that role until Grant became supreme commander in March 1864.

After the war, Halleck commanded military jurisdictions in San Francisco and Louisville, Kentucky. He died in Louisville in 1872.

GEN. WADE HAMPTON.

WADE HAMPTON

Southern generals sometimes are perceived as aristocratic planters who rode off loftily into battle. For the most part, this portrayal was inaccurate. But Wade Hampton was a plantation owner from South Carolina's high society who became widely respected as a cavalry commander.

The Charleston native was born in 1818 and was educated at South Carolina College. He was a state legislator when the secession began.

One of the South's wealthiest landowners, he equipped the "Hampton Legion" with his own resources and led the men at the First Battle of Bull Run. The legion later entered Gen. James Longstreet's command. By summer 1862, Hampton was a brigadier general and second-in-command of Gen. J.E.B. Stuart's cavalry corps. He ultimately became commander of this cavalry troop.

One of only three "citizen officers" to become Confederate lieutenant generals, Hampton led and fought valiantly. He was wounded at First Bull Run and again at Gettysburg. As the Southern cause deteriorated, he successfully delayed Union cavalry offensives against Richmond and Petersburg, Virginia. Hampton was serving under Gen. Joseph E. Johnston when the war ended.

He found his plantations devastated—as was the entire South. During the postwar years, Hampton spent his energy trying to make his lands productive again. He was elected governor of South Carolina in 1876 and 1878 and served in the U.S. Senate from 1879 to 1891. Later, he was a railroad commissioner for six years.

Hampton died in 1902 in Columbia, South Carolina.

GEN. WINFIELD S. HANCOCK

WINFIELD S. HANCOCK

Gettysburg was a terrible battle that forged many heroes. One of the brightest was Gen. Winfield S. Hancock, who arrived on the scene early and took charge of Union deployment. His brilliant decisions and stubborn defense were instrumental in the Northern victory.

Hancock was born in Pennsylvania in 1824. After graduating from West Point, he was an Indian fighter and was cited for gallantry in the Mexican War. Joining McClellan's army in September 1861, Hancock soon demonstrated his capable leadership qualities at Sharpsburg, Fredericksburg, and especially Chancellorsville.

At Gettysburg in July of 1863, Hancock was seriously wounded in the thigh during Pickett's ill-fated charge against Hancock's command. It was the end of the year before Hancock could return to action. He later received the thanks of Congress for his role in the battle. He fought numerous battles in company with Grant during 1864: the Wilderness, Spotsylvania, and Cold Harbor, to name a few. He served despite recurring problems with the thigh wound.

Hancock continued his military career after the war. He was believed by many to be presidential material during the 1868 campaign. At the Democratic National Convention that year, he received some delegates' votes, but his bid was unsuccessful. (Ulysses S. Grant, the Republican candidate, was elected president that year.) In 1880, he was nominated by the Democratic Party and lost a close race to James A. Garfield.

Hancock died at Governors Island, New York, in 1886.

GEN. A. P. HILL.

A. P. HILL

"Reinforcements!"

In the bloodiest day of the Civil War—at Antietam, Maryland, September 17, 1862—this was a rallying cry for the army of Robert E. Lee, teetering on the brink of destruction. Gen. George B. McClellan's large Union army, pressing hard from several directions, was beginning to break the Confederate right flank by late afternoon. Suddenly, within minutes of a certain Confederate collapse, the Rebel corps of A.P. Hill arrived on the scene. Hill's soldiers were exhausted—he had force-marched them all day without reprieve. But they threw themselves into the fray and pushed back the enemy.

It was by no means a Confederate victory—only a rescue. Lee withdrew his army to Virginia, thankful the strategic loss had not been a total disaster.

Hill, born in Culpeper, Virginia, in 1825, was one of the South's star generals during the first two years of the war. A West Point graduate and veteran warrior, he led units at Williamsburg, Mechanicsville, the Second Battle of Bull Run, Fredericksburg, and Cedar Mountain. His men came to be known as "Hill's Light Division" because he typically marched them faster than other units.

Hill succeeded Stonewall Jackson in command of the Second Corps when Jackson died following the Battle of Chancellorsville. Hill himself was wounded in that campaign. In 1863, he was placed in command of a newly formed Confederate corps.

Hill was killed during the defense of Petersburg, Virginia, just days before the war ended in April 1865.

GEN. JOE. HOOKER.

JOSEPH HOOKER

J oseph Hooker, born in 1814, was a gifted officer who had trouble deciding what to do with his command—or his life. After graduating from West Point and serving splendidly in the Mexican War, he resigned from the army and made an unsuccessful attempt at farming.

After the Civil War began, the Hadley, Massachusetts, native's lot in life changed dramatically. He obtained a brigadier general's commission in the Union army, and his leadership was commendable at the early battles in northern Virginia. When Lincoln decided to replace Gen. Ambrose E. Burnside as commander of the Army of the Potomac, Hooker got the nod.

His tenure in that post was a strange mixture of military skill and timidity. Hooker fell victim to Gen. Stonewall Jackson's flank attack at Chancellorsville. The South won the battle, despite early indications that Hooker might defeat Lee's army there once and for all.

Hooker was not fired from command by Lincoln, as many of his colleagues were. He asked to be relieved, sensing a lack of support from his government. He was replaced by Gen. George G. Meade shortly before the Battle of Gettysburg.

Sent to the western front, Hooker served well in Tennessee and Georgia. He apparently was snubbed for promotion by his commanding officer, Gen. William T. Sherman. Bitter, Hooker again requested relief from command.

He held several postwar military posts until 1868, when he retired because of a stroke. He died in 1879 in Garden City, New York.

GEN. STONEWALL JACKSON

STONEWALL JACKSON

To the South, Stonewall Jackson was more than a daring general. He was a legend. Jackson led his men boldly and almost always won, often against vastly superior forces. Lee, the Southern commander, referred to Jackson as his right arm. Historians still debate whether the Confederacy might have survived longer, or even won the war, had Jackson not died at the midpoint of the Civil War, after the Battle of Chancellorsville in 1863.

Born in western Virginia in 1824, Thomas Jonathan Jackson was orphaned before he turned five. Relatives raised him on a large farm and sent him to West Point, where he was a diligent but not brilliant student. After serving as an artillery officer in the Mexican War, he settled in Lexington, Virginia, and taught at Virginia Military Institute.

Jackson hoped the Union would not break apart, but when Virginia joined the Confederacy, he dutifully became an officer in gray. He was a modest man who rode an old horse and rarely removed his sword from its scabbard. But he quickly became feared by the North and adored by his soldiers, the "Stonewall Brigade"—even though he drove them so hard they were known as "foot cavalry."

His greatest victories occurred during the Shenandoah Valley campaign and at the Second Battle of Bull Run. He was a hero at Antietam, despite the Rebels' ultimate withdrawal from the field.

During the Chancellorsville conflict, Jackson mistakenly was shot by his own sentries as he returned in darkness to Confederate lines. He died of pneumonia while recovering from his wounds.

GEN. JOE. JOHNSTON.

JOSEPH E. JOHNSTON

Robert E. Lee is remembered as the commander of the Confederate army, but Lee actually commanded only part of the Rebel troops. Before Lee took over the Army of Northern Virginia, the South had another fine leader: Gen. Joseph Eggleston Johnston. In fact, Johnston's Rebels continued to fight for two weeks after Lee surrendered in 1865.

Johnston was born in Farmville, Virginia, in 1807. After graduating from West Point, he fought Indians on the frontier. He won praise and promotion for his service in the Mexican War.

At the beginning of the Civil War, Johnston was instrumental in the Southern victory at First Bull Run. In November 1862 he was given command of the South's Army of the West. For much of the war, his forces were pitted against those of Union generals Ulysses S. Grant and then William T. Sherman in the western theater.

On poor terms with Confederate president Jefferson Davis, Johnston was relieved of command in July 1864. Davis had no confidence that Johnston could save the threatened city of Atlanta. Actually, Confederate resources were simply inadequate, no matter who was in command.

Lee placed Johnston back in command of the Army of Tennessee in February 1865. By that time, there was little to be done but fight delaying actions until the inevitable surrender.

A businessman, Johnston was elected to two terms in the U.S. House of Representatives. President Grover Cleveland appointed him commissioner of railroads. Johnston died in 1891 in Washington, D.C.

GEN. SIDNEY JOHNSTON.

SIDNEY JOHNSTON

Like Stonewall Jackson and J.E.B. Stuart, Southerner Albert Sidney Johnston was killed in battle, depriving the Confederacy of an important military talent at a critical time.

Born in Washington, Kentucky, in 1803, Johnston was a West Point graduate who fought Indians on the frontier, then fought for Texas' independence in 1836. Interestingly, he joined the Texas army as a private—and rose to become the Texas army's commander in less than a year! He then was appointed secretary of war of the new Republic of Texas. Later, he fought with the American cavalry in the West. At the beginning of the Civil War, he commanded the U.S. Army's Department of the Pacific.

Confederate president Jefferson Davis placed him in charge of much of the Confederate army and ordered him to protect the South's western states. Johnston's men were driven from Fort Henry and Fort Donelson, losing important territory. But in April 1862, Johnston initiated the Battle of Shiloh. He was successful at first, catching Union Gen. Ulysses S. Grant off-guard. However, Johnston bled to death after being shot in the leg. Grant, supported by reinforcements, went on to win the battle—one of the war's bloodiest—which effectively decided the war in the West.

Whether Johnston could have contributed substantially to the Confederate cause will never be known. Grant thought Johnston overrated and unable to make clutch decisions. Davis, however, mourned him as one of the greatest generals in the Confederacy.

GEN. KILPATRICK.

JUDSON KILPATRICK

G en. Judson Kilpatrick is believed to have been the first regular army officer to receive a wound in the Civil War. It occurred at Big Bethel, Virginia, in a skirmish six weeks before the First Battle of Bull Run. Like the debacle at Bull Run, this engagement resulted in the retreat of inexperienced Union soldiers.

The Deckertown, New Jersey, native was only 25 years old and still a cadet at West Point when the Civil War began. Kilpatrick became captain of a New York Zouave unit at Little Bethel. During 1862–63, he fought in many battles in Virginia, including Brandy Station, Haymarket, and the Second Battle of Bull Run. He led a cavalry division at Gettysburg and was criticized for an ill-conceived charge. Kilpatrick rose to the rank of brigadier general, although some believe his promotions resulted at least partly from political influence. Kilpatrick is remembered as an ambitious, and at times reckless, officer who lacked self-discipline.

In February and early March 1864, Kilpatrick obtained permission to raid the Confederate capital of Richmond, Virginia, hoping to free Union prisoners and spread amnesty proclamations. His forces got through Confederate pickets outside the city, but they found Richmond too strongly defended, and withdrew.

Transferred to Sherman's western command, he was wounded again during the Atlanta campaign. He recovered and participated in Sherman's infamous "March to the Sea."

An unsuccessful candidate for Congress, Kilpatrick became U.S. minister to Chile after the war. He died in Santiago, Chile, in December 1881.

GEN. FITZHUGH LEE.

FITZHUGH LEE

Probably the second most famous Lee in the Civil War was Fitzhugh, Robert E. Lee's nephew. The Confederate commander in chief's two oldest sons, Custis and Rooney, both became Confederate generals; their younger brother, Robert Jr., was a captain. But their cousin Fitzhugh earned the greatest reputation as a superb cavalry officer.

Fitzhugh, born in Fairfax County, Virginia, in 1835, would become one of the war's youngest generals. For a time, however, it seemed doubtful he would finish West Point. Bad behavior brought him within a whisker of being expelled by his uncle Robert, who was superintendent of the academy. Fitzhugh graduated far down in his class.

Before the Civil War began, Fitzhugh was wounded in the Indian wars. Then he returned to West Point to become a tactics instructor. When Virginia seceded from the Union, he joined the Southern army.

Fitzhugh fought under Gen. J.E.B. Stuart in 1862. By the end of the war he had participated in many of the major battles, including Antietam, Chancellorsville, Gettysburg, and Spotsylvania. He ended his Civil War career as the senior cavalry officer in the Army of Northern Virginia.

After the war, he changed from dashing cavalier to ordinary farmer, but later he was elected governor of Virginia. Then he was appointed consul-general to Cuba. And his fighting days were not over! At the outbreak of the Spanish-American War—three decades after the Civil War had ended—Fitzhugh Lee was given a major general's commission in the U.S. Army. He served well in Cuba, retiring in 1901. He died four years later in Washington, D.C.

GEN. ROBERT E. LEE.

ROBERT E. LEE

I f President Lincoln had had his way, Robert E. Lee of Virginia would have commanded the Union armies. After the conflict began at Fort Sumter, in April 1861, Lincoln offered command to Lee, a brilliant cavalry officer and former superintendent of West Point. Lee declined, feeling bound to serve his home state when it entered the Confederacy.

Lee was born in 1807 in Westmoreland County, Virginia. His father, "Light Horse Harry" Lee, was a hero of the American Revolution. After graduating with top honors from West Point, Robert E. Lee married Mary Custis, a descendant of First Lady Martha Washington.

Before returning to West Point as superintendent in 1852, Lee earned glory in the Mexican War, where he was wounded. He was serving in the U.S. cavalry in Texas when the Southern states began to secede, and he returned to Virginia. After turning down Lincoln's offer, he took command of Virginia's forces. A year later he was named commander of the primary Rebel military force, which he named the Army of Northern Virginia.

For almost three years he sparred with the Union Army of the Potomac in some of history's bloodiest battles. Much of his overall strategy was defensive, intended to protect the eastern Confederate states from Union occupation, but he also launched daring offensives into Northern territory. Lee surrendered his army to Gen. Ulysses S. Grant at Appomattox, Virginia, in April 1865, signaling the end of the Civil War.

Lee sought to quell the bitterness left by the war as president of Washington College in Lexington, Virginia. He died in 1870, respected by both Southerners and Northerners.

GEN. JAMES LONGSTREET

JAMES LONGSTREET

amilies and comrades were split by the American Civil War. A pleasant exception was the lifelong friendship of Union Gen. Ulysses S. Grant and Confederate Gen. James Longstreet. They met at West Point and served together at an army post in Missouri during the 1840s. While there, Grant met and married Longstreet's cousin, Julia Dent.

Wounded in the Mexican War, Longstreet, a South Carolina native, later was an administrative officer in the Southwest. He was there when the Civil War began, and he resigned from the U.S. Army and was commissioned a Confederate brigadier general.

Longstreet's unit entered combat at the First Battle of Bull Run. He immediately proved his courage, rallying inexperienced soldiers in the thick of battle when they began to falter. Throughout the war, he was a master of defensive fighting. He often hesitated, however, in offensive endeavors. This tendency was especially notable at the Second Battle of Bull Run and at Gettysburg. Some historians believe his delayed attack at Gettysburg was at least part of the reason for the Confederate defeat, though Longstreet himself blamed Lee's overall strategy.

Nevertheless, Longstreet became one of Lee's most trusted generals. "My old warhorse," Lee called him. Wounded in 1864 during the Wilderness campaign, Longstreet missed half a year's action. He returned to action as Lee's army was being hounded toward final defeat at Appomattox.

After the war, he renewed his old friendship with Grant and served as U.S. minister to Turkey. He died in 1904 at Gainesville, Georgia.

GEN. GEO.B. McCLELLAN.

GEORGE B. McCLELLAN

When President Lincoln sensed a need to replace Gen. Irvin McDowell, the Union commander, after the loss at First Bull Run, he looked to Gen. George B. McClellan. McClellan was very popular in the military. Second in his graduating class at West Point, he had been promoted twice in Mexico.

McClellan succeeded in training a capable, impressive Army of the Potomac. But his field leadership was marked by mistakes and poor judgment—and by blaming the government for lack of support. In the frenzy of one battle disaster, he wired Secretary of War Edwin M. Stanton: "If I save this army now, I tell you plainly that I owe no thanks to you or to any other persons in Washington. You have done your best to sacrifice this army."

McClellan was replaced in overall command by Gen. Ambrose E. Burnside in November 1862. This was less than two months after McClellan allowed Lee's army to escape at the Battle of Antietam.

George Brinton McClellan, born in 1826 at Philadelphia, was a studious soldier. He had observed European army strategy and tactics in the Crimean War, and he brought back from Hungary the concept for a unique cavalry saddle, which became standard equipment in the U.S. Army. McClellan demonstrated a gift for strategy, but not for overall command.

After losing his command, McClellan did not participate in the war. He was the unsuccessful Democratic candidate against Lincoln in the 1864 presidential elections. Later he served as governor of New Jersey. He died in 1885.

GEN. IRVIN McDOWELL.

IRVIN McDOWELL

Irvin McDowell was in the wrong place at the wrong time. The place was Manassas Junction, Virginia, the time was July 21, 1861, and the newly organized Union army under his command was overconfident and quite unprepared for the First Battle of Bull Run.

Born in Ohio in 1818 and educated in France, McDowell had served in the Mexican War and on the American frontier after graduating from West Point. Placed in command of the Union army by President Lincoln, McDowell was expected to advance on Richmond, the Confederate capital, and end the war quickly.

It was a wonderful honor to be given such trust, but it was an impossible task. Neither the Union nor the Confederate army was prepared to execute well in what history calls the "battle of amateurs." Furthermore, McDowell's movements before the First Battle of Bull Run were observed by the Confederates. The fight was a confusion of miscommunication and mistaken identities. In the end, it was the Yankees who fled the field in disarray.

Although McDowell could not be fully blamed, he was replaced by Gen. George B. McClellan. McDowell was given lesser commands for the next year. After the Second Battle of Bull Run in August 1862, McDowell was held partly responsible for the Union defeat and was removed from field command for the rest of the war.

After commanding several regional military departments after the war, McDowell retired from service in 1882. He died three years later in San Francisco.

GEN. G.G. MEADE.

G. G. MEADE

en. George Gordon Meade was born in Spain in 1815, son of a U.S. Navy official. He graduated from West Point and served in Florida during the Seminole War. Cited for bravery during the Mexican War, he was an army surveyor and engineer until the Civil War began.

Early in the war, Meade was involved in the defense of Washington, D.C., and in actions in Virginia. He was seriously wounded at the Battle of White Oak Swamp in June 1862, and he earned praise for his roles at the Second Battle of Bull Run and Antietam.

Recognized as an aggressive, effective leader, Meade was named commander of the Army of the Potomac—somewhat against his wishes—just before the crucial Battle of Gettysburg. He orchestrated the Union victory, which became a turning point in the Civil War.

When President Lincoln placed Gen. Ulysses S. Grant in command of all the Union armies, Grant set up his headquarters with the Army of the Potomac. Meade officially continued to command that force until the end of the war, although Grant was popularly recognized as the Union chief. Meade's role, at least to appearances, became secondary. However, Meade was commended by Grant and is regarded as one of the Union's best generals.

Meade served in Atlanta after the war as a military administrator during Reconstruction, and he was recognized as a sensitive director of occupation policies. He died in 1872 at Philadelphia.

GEN PHIL.H.SHERIDAN.

PHILIP H. SHERIDAN

"Fighting Phil" was Gen. Philip Sheridan's nickname. He earned the reputation not just by his remarkable exploits but by the sheer length of his record: Philip Henry Sheridan was a professional soldier from his youth as a West Point cadet until his death at age 57.

Sheridan was born to Irish parents in Albany, New York, in 1831. His years at West Point were marred by suspension for chasing a fellow cadet with a bayonet. He graduated inconspicuously and served with the army on the Texas frontier in the mid-1850s. His escape from Apache captors amid a storm of arrows became an army legend.

Such feats were to become commonplace for Sheridan, who was considered a fine officer during the Civil War. He was aggressive in action and insisted on leading his troops into battle. He rose quickly in rank. In 1864 he was given command of the cavalry of the Army of the Potomac. Later that year he was named commander of the Army of the Shenandoah. Among other successes, he personally turned defeat into victory at Cedar Creek by rallying his troops against Confederate Gen. Jubal Early's surprise attack.

When Grant became president after the war, he made Sheridan a lieutenant general and gave him important post-war assignments. Eventually, Sheridan became commander in chief of the U.S. Army.

Like many fellow heroes in blue, Sheridan probably could have ridden his fame into political office. He refused, preferring to remain a soldier all his life. He died in 1888 in Nosquitt, Massachusetts.

GEN. W. T. SHERMAN.

W.T. SHERMAN

To this day, Gen. William Tecumseh Sherman's name is loathed in the South. That's because of his army's fiery, plundering "March to the Sea" through the Southeast near the end of the war. Sherman, however, was unquestionably one of the war's most capable commanders. His military record is not brilliant, but he was tenaciously effective.

Sherman was born in 1820 in Ohio. He graduated high in his West Point class, then fought commendably in California during the Mexican War. At the beginning of the Civil War, he was a brigadier general, ranking ahead of Ulysses S. Grant on the U.S. War Department's list of generals. He was temperamental, offending reporters who, he thought, probed unnecessarily into highly sensitive military matters. He fought primarily in the western theater, ultimately being given overall command there.

It was as the western commander that he drove Gen. Joseph E. Johnston's Confederates from Tennessee to Atlanta. After the capture of that city, Sherman directed his army's 40-mile-wide "March to the Sea." They descended upon Savannah at the end of 1864, then ravaged the land as they passed northward through the Carolinas. Sherman's idea of "modern warfare" included the belief that civilians bore some of the responsibility for their soldiers' actions and thus he believed that Southern citizens deserved punishment.

Grant appointed Sherman commander in chief of the U.S. Army after Grant's election to the White House in 1868. Sherman retired from the military in 1884 and died in New York City in 1891.

GEN. J.E.B. STUART.

J. E. B. STUART

His colleagues sometimes wondered about his independent yearnings, but James Ewell Brown "Jeb" Stuart consistently demonstrated boldness, skill, and intelligence as the Confederacy's premier cavalry commander.

Born in Patrick County, Virginia, in 1833, Stuart graduated from West Point and served in Kansas before the Civil War. He accompanied then-Lt. Col. Robert E. Lee in the prewar capture of abolitionist guerrilla fighter John Brown at Harper's Ferry, Virginia. Stuart became a Virginia cavalry commander when the states went to war. He initially served in the Shenandoah Valley under Gen. Joseph E. Johnston.

After his noble performance at the First Battle of Bull Run, Stuart became a brigadier general. He further proved his salt by riding all the way around Gen. George B. McClellan's Army of the Potomac to scout the Yankees' position before the Seven Days battles. Lee named him cavalry commander of the Army of Northern Virginia in summer 1862.

In battle after battle, Stuart showed his mettle. He was the "eyes and ears of Lee's army" as well as an excellent warrior and tactician. He often roamed at large, boldly surveying enemy positions. At times even his own superiors did not know where he was. The Confederates needed him badly at Gettysburg, but he arrived too late in the three-day battle to affect the outcome—a pivotal Union victory. The main reason for Stuart's delay was his capture of 125 Union supply wagons in Maryland. To many Southerners, Stuart was a primary scapegoat for the loss at Gettysburg.

Stuart died after being shot at the Battle of Yellow Tavern near Richmond in May 1864.

GEN. G. H. THOMAS.

G. H. THOMAS

en. George Henry Thomas is remembered as "the Rock of Chickamauga." He earned the nickname when his command held their position against formidable Confederate forces at the Battle of Chickamauga in Tennessee in 1863, one of the last major Confederate victories. While most of his comrades retreated, Thomas stubbornly anchored the Union left flank until his men could make an orderly withdrawal.

Thomas was born in Southampton County, Virginia, in 1816. He served his country in the Seminole and Mexican wars and taught at West Point. Naturally, as a Virginian, it was difficult for him to choose which side to fight for when war broke out. Against the wishes of many family members and friends, he remained with the U.S. Army.

Thomas first fought in the Shenandoah Valley, then was transferred to the western theater of the war, where he participated in such battles as Shiloh and Perryville. After his heroics at Chickamauga, he was promoted to brigadier general and was given command of the Army of the Cumberland.

After the war, Thomas commanded the Military Division of the Pacific. He died while serving in that role in San Francisco in 1870. He, like Gen. Winfield S. Hancock, was one of the few Union officers to receive the official thanks of Congress. This recognition was for his part in the fighting at Franklin and Nashville. It was a fitting tribute, for until late in the war, many of Thomas' fellow officers questioned his allegiance to the Union.

CHRONOLOGY

November 6, 1860 - Abraham Lincoln is elected president of the United States.

December 20, 1860 - South Carolina becomes the first state to secede from the Union. Other Southern states follow, forming the Confederate States of America.

April 12, 1861 - Fighting begins with the bombardment of Fort Sumter in Charleston Harbor, South Carolina. U.S. forces relinquish the fort with minor casualties.

July 21, 1861 - The South wins the war's first major battle at Bull Run (Manassas), Virginia.

April 6-7, 1862 - Grant and Buell win the Battle of Shiloh in Tennessee, a decisive Union victory in the western theater.

August 29-30, 1862 - Confederates win the Second Battle of Bull Run.

September 17, 1862 - The Battle of Antietam in Maryland, bloodiest day of the war. McClellan's Army of the Potomac wins marginally—but should have won decisively, in the opinion of some historians. A popular song lyric of the day was, "The Yanks gained the day, but the Rebs got away. . . ."

September 22, 1862 - President Lincoln issues the Emancipation Proclamation, demanding that slaves be freed.

December 13, 1862 - Gen. A.E. Burnside's Army of the Potomac unsuccessfully attacks Lee's army at Fredericksburg with great loss of life.

May 1-4, 1863 - Stonewall Jackson plays a vital role in the South's victory at Chancellorsville—and suffers a mortal wound in the process.

July 1-3, 1863 - Lee's invasion of Pennsylvania is halted at the Battle of Gettysburg. Some historians consider this battle the turning point of the war in the east.

July 3, 1863 - The Confederate stronghold at Vicksburg, Mississippi, on the Mississippi River surrenders after a long siege.

November 19, 1863 - President Lincoln delivers the Gettysburg Address.

May 5-7, 1864 - The Battle of the Wilderness, Virginia. It is a strategic victory for the North, as Grant's army gradually pressures Lee from northern Virginia.

September 1-2, 1864 - Sherman's army captures and burns Atlanta.

April 3, 1865 - The Confederate capital of Richmond is captured and burned.

April 9, 1865 - Lee and Grant discuss terms of peace at Appomattox, Virginia.

April 12, 1865 - Lee's army surrenders to Grant.

April 15, 1865 - President Lincoln is assassinated in Washington, D.C.

April 26, 1865 - Gen. Joseph E. Johnston surrenders his portion of the Confederate army to Gen. William T. Sherman.

INDEX

49, 51

Longstreet, Gen. James, 25, 45

McClellan, Gen. George B., 13, 23,
   27, 29, 47, 49, 57

McDowell, Gen. Irvin, 47, 49

"March to the Sea", 39, 55

Meade, Gen. George G., 31, 51

Mechanicsville, Battle of, 29

Mexican War, 11, 13, 21, 23, 27, 31,
   33, 43, 45, 47, 49, 51, 55, 59

Monocacy, Battle of, 17

Nashville, Battle of, 59

New Orleans (surrender of), 15

Perryville, Battle of, 59

Pickett's Charge (Gettysburg), 27

Pope, Gen. John, 23

Porter, Adm. David Dixon, 15

Revolutionary War, 43

Richmond and Petersburg defenses,
   19, 25, 29, 39

Seven Days battles, 57

Shenandoah Valley campaigns, 17, 33,
   57, 59

Sheridan, Gen. Philip H., 17, 53

Sherman, Gen. William T., 15, 21, 31,
   35, 39, 55

Shiloh, Battle of, 11, 21, 37, 59

Spanish-American War, 41

Spotsylvania, Battle of, 19, 27, 41

Stanton, Edwin M., 47

Stuart, Gen. J.E.B., 25, 37, 41, 57

Texas, Republic of, 37

Thomas, Gen. G.H., 59

Vicksburg, siege of, 21

Wallace, Gen. Lew, 17

Washington, D.C., defenses, 51

Washington, Martha, 43

Welles, Gideon, 23

West Point (United States Military
   Academy), 11, 13, 17, 19, 23, 27,
   29, 31, 33, 35, 37, 39, 41, 43, 45,
   47, 49, 51, 53, 55, 57, 59

White Oak Swamp, Battle of, 51

Wilderness, Battle of the, 27, 45

Williamsburg, Battle of, 17, 29

Yellow Tavern, Battle of, 57

FURTHER READING

Anders, Curt. *Fighting Confederates*. New York: Dorset Press, 1968.

Boatner, Mark Mayo, III. *The Civil War Dictionary*. New York: David McKay Company, Inc., 1959.

Davis, William C., *et al*, eds. *Civil War Journal: The Leaders*. Nashville: Rutledge Hill Press, Inc., 1997.

Faust, Patricia L., ed. *Historical Times Illustrated Encyclopedia of the Civil War*. New York: HarperCollins Publishers, 1986.

Glatthaar, Joseph T. *Partners in Command: The Relationships Between Leaders in the Civil War*. New York: The Free Press (A Division of Macmillan, Inc.), 1994.

Mitchell, Lt. Col. Joseph B. *Military Leaders in the Civil War*. New York: G.P. Putnam's Sons, 1972.

Tracey, Patrick Austin. *Military Leaders of the Civil War*. New York: Facts on File, Inc., 1993.

Warner, Ezra J. *Generals in Blue: Lives of the Union Commanders*. Baton Rouge: Louisiana State University Press, 1964.

_____. *Generals in Gray: Lives of the Confederate Commanders*. Baton Rouge: Louisiana State University Press, 1959.